From the series "Scripture and Feasts for Children"

A Children's Prayer Book

Illustrations by Olga Podivilova
Commentary by Elena Trostnikova

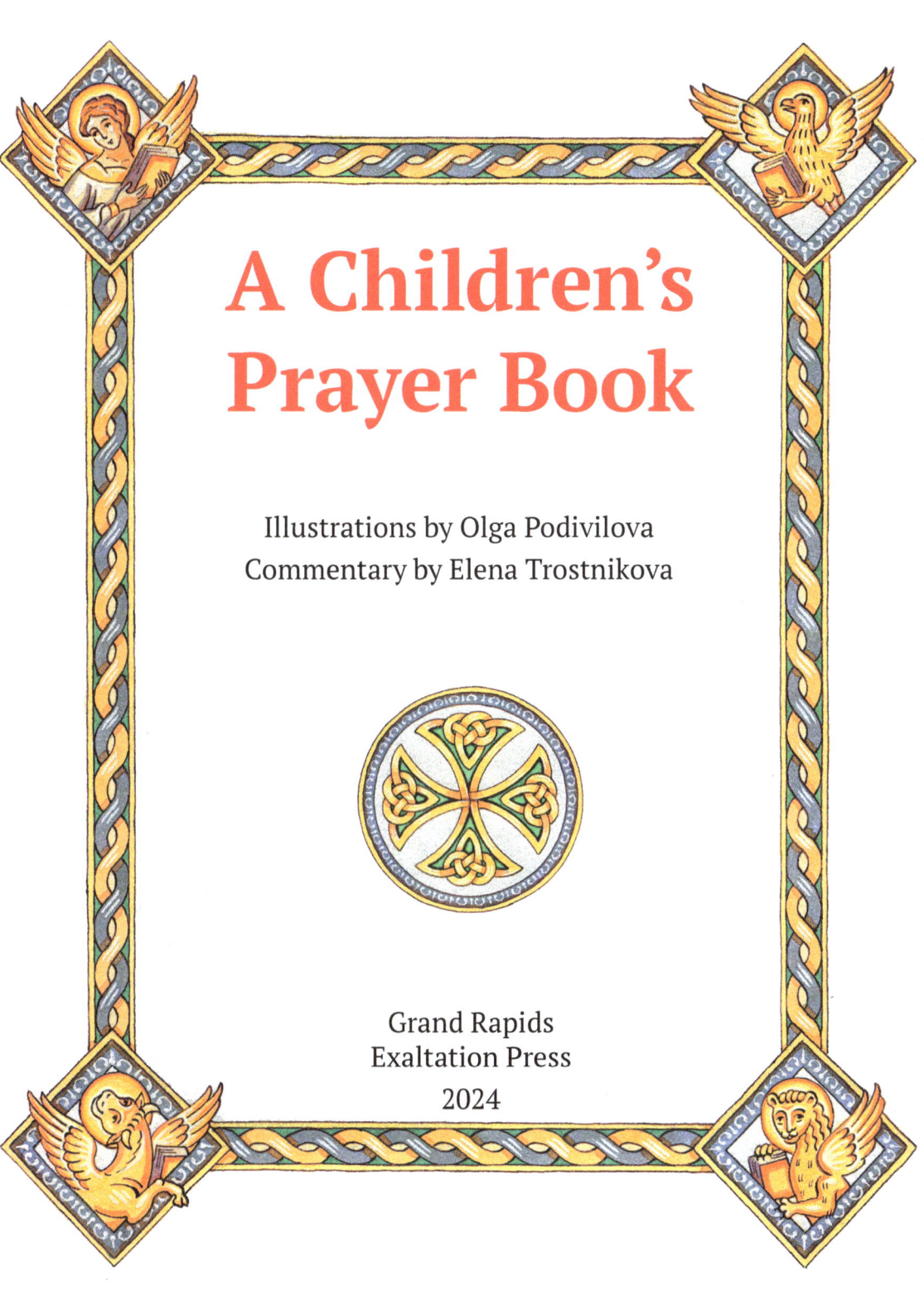

Grand Rapids
Exaltation Press
2024

Copyright © 2024 Exaltation Press

Author: Elena Trostnikova
Illustrator: Olga Podivilova
Translator: Fr. John Hogg

"A Children's Prayer Book"
    This book is part of the series "Scripture and Feasts for Children." Unlike the other books in the series that tell about the life of Christ through the Gospel narratives, this book is designed as a first prayer book for young children. Using illustrations to accompany the prayers, it seeks to engage the attention of children from a very early age.
    It also contains advice to parents on how to teach their children to pray, suggested modifications for young children, and explanations of the meanings of some of the prayers.

All rights reserved. This book or any portion thereof may not be reproduced or used in any manner whatsoever without the express written permission of the publisher except for the use of brief quotations in a book review.

Translated from the original "Молитвослов для детей с объяснением молитв" by Nikea Press, Copyright © Trading House «NIKEA», www.Nikeabooks.ru

ISBN: 978-1-950067-18-3 (Paperback)

First printing edition 2024

Exaltation Press
Grand Rapids, MI

www.ExaltationPress.com

For bulk orders, please contact editor@exaltationpress.com

Help us build our permanent temple for future generations! Scan this QR-code to donate to Holy Cross Antiochian Orthodox Church in Grand Rapids, MI. Thank you and God bless you!

Table of Contents

Introduction: Prayer is a conversation with God 9

MORNING PRAYERS 11

Opening Prayers 11
Prayer to the Holy Spirit 11
The Trisagion 12
Prayer to the All-Holy Trinity 12
The Lord's Prayer 14
Prayer to the Most-Holy Theotokos 17
Prayer to Your Guardian Angel 19
Prayer to the Saint Whose Name You Bear 19
Prayer for Your Parents 19
Prayer for the Living 20
Prayer for the Reposed 21
Closing Prayers 22

EVENING PRAYERS 25

A Prayer for Forgiveness 27
Another Prayer to Your Guardian Angel 27
Another Prayer to the Most-holy Theotokos 28
Closing Prayers 28
Prayer Before Sleep 29

PRAYERS FOR VARIOUS OCCASIONS 30

Prayer Before Eating 30
Prayer After Eating 31
Prayer Before Beginning Any Task 33
Prayer After Finishing a Task 33
Prayer Before Studying 33
Prayer of the Elders of Optina 34
From the Prayers Before Communion 36
From the Prayers of Thanksgiving After Holy Communion 37
The Jesus Prayer 39

How to teach children to pray 40

Explanations of the Prayers 45

с.4

Introduction
Prayer is a conversation with God

God created the whole world and each of us. God loves His world and us, His people. He loves you and me and He rejoices that we are His and wants us to rejoice in Him, in each other, and in the life He gives us.

Just like we don't see the air we breathe, but depend on it to live, so also, although we don't see God with our physical eyes, we receive our whole life from Him. God always sees us, loves us, and helps us. God wants us to remember Him and He wants us to be able to talk with Him, to find joy in Him, to give Him thanks and to share with Him everything that is on our hearts, to ask His help. If we do something wrong, He wants us to ask His forgiveness.

We can talk to God with our own words. He will hear us and kind of prayer is important. But talking to God is a special kind of conversation, not like talking with the people around us. There are special words to you, words from the saints, who knew God and were close to Him. Every day, a great multitude of people turn to God using these words and it becomes one common prayer. Using these prayers that have been given to us will let us join in with that prayer, together with all the rest!

Elena Trostnikova

Morning Prayers

In everything that we do, we need God's help. And so, as soon as you wake up, stand reverently, remembering that you stand before God who sees all things, make the sign of the Cross and say:

In the Name of the Father, and of the Son, and of the Holy Spirit.
Amen.

Opening Prayers

(This is how both morning and evening prayers begin)

O Lord Jesus Christ, Son of God, for the sake of the prayers of Thy most pure Mother and of all the saints, have mercy on us.
Amen.
Glory to thee, our God, glory to Thee.

Prayer to the Holy Spirit

O heavenly King, O Comforter, the Spirit of truth, who art in all places and fillest all things; Treasury of good things and Giver of life: Come and dwell in us and cleanse us from every stain, and save our souls, O Good One.

The Trisagion

Holy God, Holy Mighty, Holy Immortal, have mercy on us.
(This is said three times, with the sign of the cross and a bow each time.)

Glory to the Father, and to the Son, and to the Holy Spirit both now and ever, and unto ages of ages.
Amen.

Prayer to the All-Holy Trinity

All-holy Trinity, have mercy on us. Lord, cleanse us from our sins. Master, pardon our iniquities. Holy One, visit and heal our infirmities for thy Name's sake.

Lord, have mercy. Lord, have mercy. Lord, have mercy.

Glory to the Father, and to the Son, and to the Holy Spirit both now and ever, and unto ages of ages.
Amen.

The Lord's Prayer

Our Father, who art in heaven, hallowed be thy Name; thy kingdom come; thy will be done on earth, as it is in heaven. Give us this day our daily bread; and forgive us our trespasses, as we forgive those who trespass against us; and lead us not into temptation, but deliver us from the evil one.

Prayer to the Most-Holy Theotokos

O Virgin Theotokos, rejoice, O Mary, full of grace, the Lord is with Thee. Blessed art Thou among women and blessed is the fruit of Thy womb for Thou has born the Savior of our souls.

Prayer to Your Guardian Angel

O Angel of God, my holy guardian, sent to me by God from Heaven for my salvation! I fervently pray thee: Enlighten me this day and preserve me from all evil. Teach me to do what is good and lead me onto the path of salvation. Amen.

Prayer to the Saint Whose Name You Bear

Pray to God for me, O holy God-pleasing Saint (Name), for I fervently run to thee, the speedy helper and intercessor for my soul.

Prayer for Your Parents

Save, O Lord, and have mercy on my parents. Grant them unity of mind and firm love all the days of their lives and health of body and soul. Help me to love and obey them and teach me to honor them according to their commandment and to bring them joy. Keep me from all lying and deception towards them and from causing them distress. Make our family into a little Church so that we may glorify Thee together, our Lord Jesus Christ. Amen.

Prayer for the Living

Save, O Lord, and have mercy on my spiritual father *(name)*, my parents *(names)*, my relatives, those in authority, my teachers and benefactors, and all Orthodox Christians.

_____   _____

_____   _____

_____   _____

_____   _____

_____   _____

_____   _____

Prayer for the Reposed

Give rest, O Lord, to the souls of Thy servants who have fallen asleep: my relatives and benefactors (names) and all Orthodox Christians, and forgive them all their transgressions, willing and unwilling, and grant them Thy Heavenly Kingdom.

_____   _____

_____   _____

_____   _____

_____   _____

_____   _____

_____   _____

Closing Prayers

It is truly meet to bless thee, O Theotokos, who art ever blessed and all-blameless, and the mother of our God. More honorable than the Cherubim, and more glorious beyond compare than the Seraphim, thou who without stain barest God the Word, and art truly Theotokos: we magnify thee.

Glory to the Father, and the Son, and the Holy Spirit, both now and ever and unto ages of ages. Amen.

Lord, have mercy. Lord, have mercy. Lord, have mercy.

O Lord Jesus Christ, Son of God, through the prayers of Thine All-holy Mother, of our venerable and God-bearing Fathers, and of all the saints, have mercy on us. Amen.

Evening Prayers

Just like we should pray when we wake up in the morning, we should also pray and give thanks to God before going to bed. Make sure to pray before you are too tired to pay attention. Begin like with morning prayers by crossing yourself and saying:

In the Name of the Father, and of the Son, and of the Holy Spirit.
Amen.

O Lord Jesus Christ, Son of God, for the sake of the prayers of Thy most pure Mother and of all the saints, have mercy on us.
Amen.
Glory to thee, our God, glory to Thee.

O heavenly King, O Comforter, the Spirit of truth, who art in all places and fillest all things; Treasury of good things and Giver of life: Come and dwell in us and cleanse us from every stain, and save our souls, O Good One.

Holy God, Holy Mighty, Holy Immortal, have mercy on us.
(This is said three times, with the sign of the cross and a bow each time.)

Glory to the Father, and to the Son, and to the Holy Spirit both now and ever, and unto ages of ages. Amen.

All-holy Trinity, have mercy on us. Lord, cleanse us from our sins. Master, pardon our iniquities. Holy One, visit and heal our infirmities for thy Name's sake.

Lord, have mercy. Lord, have mercy. Lord, have mercy.

Glory to the Father, and to the Son, and to the Holy Spirit both now and ever, and unto ages of ages.
Amen.

Our Father, who art in heaven, hallowed be thy Name; thy kingdom come; thy will be done on earth, as it is in heaven. Give us this day our daily bread; and forgive us our trespasses, as we forgive those who trespass against us; and lead us not into temptation, but deliver us from the evil one.

A Prayer for Forgiveness

O Lord our God, if I have sinned this day in word, deed, or thought, forgive me, since Thou art good and lovest mankind. Give thou me a peaceful and undisturbed sleep. Send me Thy guardian angel to cover and keep me from all evil, for Thou art the guardian of our souls and bodies and unto Thee we send up glory, to the Father, and the Son, and the Holy Spirit, always now and ever and unto ages of ages. Amen.

Another Prayer to Your Guardian Angel

O Angel of Christ, my holy guardian and the protector of my soul and body, forgive me everything in which I have sinned this day and deliver me from all craftiness of the enemy so that I may not anger my God by any sin. Pray thou for me, thy sinful and unworthy servant that I may be shown worthy of the goodness and mercy the All-holy Trinity, the Mother of my Lord Jesus Christ, and of all the saints. Amen.

Another Prayer to the Most-holy Theotokos

To Thee the Champion Leader, we Thy servants ascribe thanksgiving as ones delivered from evils, O Theotokos, but since Thou hast invincible power deliver us from all sorrows that we may call out to Thee: Rejoice, O Unwedded Bride.

Closing Prayers

It is truly meet to bless thee, O Theotokos, who art ever blessed and all-blameless, and the mother of our God. More honorable than the Cherubim, and more glorious beyond compare than the Seraphim, thou who without stain barest God the Word, and art truly Theotokos: we magnify thee.

Glory to the Father, and the Son, and the Holy Spirit, both now and ever and unto ages of ages. Amen.

Lord, have mercy. Lord, have mercy. Lord, have mercy.

O Lord Jesus Christ, Son of God, through the prayers of Thine All-holy Mother, of our venerable and God-bearing Fathers, and of all the saints, have mercy on us. Amen.

Prayer Before Sleep

Into Thy hands, O Lord Jesus Christ, I commend my spirit. Bless me, have mercy on me, and grant me eternal life.
    Amen.

Prayers for Various Occasions

Prayer Before Eating

One person should read the Lord's Prayer ("Our Father") or everyone can sing it together. Then, the eldest, or the person he designates, making the sign of the Cross on himself and then over the table with the food, saying:

Through the prayers of our holy fathers, O Lord, bless the food and drink of Thy servants. Amen.

Prayer After Eating

We thank Thee, O Christ our God, for having satisfied us with Thine earthly blessings. Deprive us not of Thy Heavenly Kingdom, but as Thou didst come to Thy disciples, O Savior, and grant them peace, so come to us and save us!

Prayer Before Beginning Any Task

O Lord, bless me!

Or:

Bless me, O Lord, and help me to complete the task I have begun to Thy glory.

Prayer After Finishing a Task

Glory to Thee, O Lord, glory to Thee!

Or:

Thou art the fulfillment of all good things, O my Christ. Fill my soul with joy and gladness and save me, since Thou alone art most merciful, O Lord, glory to Thee.

Prayer Before Studying

O Lord, help me in my studies!
Or else you can read (or sing) the prayer "O Heavenly King."

Prayer of the Elders of Optina

O Lord, grant that I may meet all that this coming day brings me with spiritual tranquility. Grant that I may fully surrender myself to Thy holy will. At every hour of this day, direct and support me in all things. Whatsoever news may reach me in the course of the day, teach me to accept it with a calm soul and the firm conviction that all is subject to Thy holy will. Direct my thoughts and feelings in all my words and actions. In all unexpected occurrences, do not let me forget that all is sent down from thee. Grant that I may deal straightforwardly and wisely with every member of my family, neither embarrassing nor saddening anyone. O Lord, grant me the strength to endure the fatigue of the coming day and all the events that take place during it. Direct my will and teach me to pray, to believe, to hope, to be patient, to forgive, and to love. Amen.

From the Prayers Before Communion

Of Thy Mystical Supper, O Son of God, receive me today as a communicant for I will not speak of Thy Mysteries to Thine enemy nor will I give Thee a kiss like Judas but like the thief I will confess Thee: Remember me, O Lord, in Thy Kingdom.

From the Prayers of Thanksgiving After Holy Communion

May Thy Holy Body, O Lord Jesus Christ our God, be to me for eternal life and Thy Precious Blood for the forgiveness of sins. May this Eucharist be to me for joy, health, and gladness. Amen.

The Jesus Prayer

Lord Jesus Christ, Son of God,
have mercy on me, a sinner.

Elena Trostnikova
How to teach children to pray

A prayer book, whether for adults or children, is not just a "book to read," but a book of action. Both this book itself and the adults who read it to children have a difficult task, to lead children into the world of prayer. For that reason, before you begin to read this book to your children, it is essential that you thoughtfully read this part of the book, addressed to you, the adult reader. You don't even necessarily have to agree with everything proposed here, but you should think it through and in some sense live it.

Like all of the books in the series "Scripture and Feasts for Children," this prayer book is addressed to very young children, who do not yet know how to read, which means that it's also addressed to their parents. When you read this book together, you'll be offering to God a common prayer.

If you read this book to your children "like a book," their reaction will be confusion and a host of questions about words and meanings that they don't understand. If, however, from the very beginning, you approach it as a way to turn to God together in prayer, as active prayer, your children will usually absorb the words completely naturally (just like children who can't yet talk absorb the speech of their elders without having to ask questions) and will absorb the movement and sounds that are done with love and faith.

Still, we should be prepared for some questions and we should first clarify those questions for ourselves so that if needed, we will be able to answer them.

Of course, all of the recommendations below are not absolute, but it's worth acquainting yourself with them and thinking them through so that you can work out your own approach for your own children.

How to read this book to very little children

The books in the series "Scripture and Feasts for Children" are designed to be read by adults to children aged two and up. It's clear, however, that the collection of prayers that a two-year-old can learn is very different from those that can be learned by, say, a five-year-old. This prayer book is somewhat designed for little kids to "grow into," and so we'll talk separately here about how to read it to those little children.

Ages two and three are the ages when a mother is a child's main school, when prayers are learned by ear and in an abbreviated form, when a simple, "Lord, have mercy on mom, dad, grandma, and Steve," is still, perhaps, a child's most important and sincere prayer.

By two years old, only certain little children are capable of mastering something as simple at first glance as the sign of the cross. You'll need to help them: fold their fingers and then help them to make the sign of the cross, using their own fingers. You'll need to repeat this over and over again, from time to time asking them to try crossing themselves independently and then gently correcting them.

Little children at first will not learn the prayer book in its entirety. Right from the beginning, though, the Lord's prayer ("Our Father") and "O Theotokos and Virgin" should be learned in full (ideally, through singing). There will need to be more conversations "around prayer" at this age as children get acquainted with the prayers than there will need to be at older ages, but those conversations should not so much be explanations of difficult truths or concepts, but rather warm words about faith and God's love and our love.

A rough plan for helping children master the prayers

On page 11, "In the name of the Father, and the Son, and the Holy

Spirit. Amen." Then, replace the following prayer with "Lord, have mercy," and "Glory to Thee, O Lord, glory to Thee." The prayer to the Holy Spirit ("O Heavenly King") will need to be introduced a little later, although it could also be introduced right away through singing it like it is sung at Molebens.

On page 12, "Glory to the Father, and the Son, and the Holy Spirit" and "Lord, have mercy." Later on, you can introduce the Trisagion.

Then, the Our Father and the prayer to the Theotokos, "O Theotokos and Virgin."

On page 19, we'll replace the prayer to the Guardian Angel and the child's patron saint with a simplified version: "O Angel of God, my Guardian, protect me!" and "Holy (name), pray to God for us!" (Preferably "for us," since it will be followed by a prayer for family members.) Then, finally, "Lord, have mercy on mom, dad, grandma…" and then put in all the names of relatives and friends, and then the children themselves will eagerly add in the names of more distant relatives, family friends, their own friends, teachers, and so on. If they want to add in the names of your pets, don't forbid them. That kind of childish prayer is also pleasing to God.

In terms of the commemoration lists, just tell your children that this is where you'll write down the names of the people that they always pray for. This will be important for them long before they learn to read and write.

For the closing prayers, (page 22), for young children, I'd suggest, "O Lord, through the prayers of the Theotokos and all the saints, have mercy on us!"

On pages 25-29, for evening prayers, in the beginning, you could begin by suggesting to them the following prayer before sleep: "O Lord, give me a peaceful sleep and send me my Guardian Angel."

If you say prayers as a family, your little ones can simply stand nearby while you, the parents, pray and add their little bows to yours and cross themselves as they are able. You could also just hold them in your arms while you pray.

Before eating (page 30), the prayer for blessing the food is the

"Our Father", but you could suggest to children that they say simply, "O Lord, bless our food." It's important to teach children to always pray after eating, "O Lord, we thank you!"

On page 33, we should tell our children that it is good to begin every good work with a short prayer: "Lord, bless this!" and that after finishing what we're doing, we shouldn't forget to glorify God by saying, "Glory to Thee, O Lord!" Nothing else is needed here.

On pages 34-35, in terms of the Elders of Optina depicted in the illustration, you can tell your children a bit about them. For example, you can tell them that there's a monastery called Optina, where there were wonderful priests who taught people goodness and prayer and who prayed for everyone. Then, teach them the ending of the prayer, "Lord, teach me to pray, to believe, to hope, to be patient, to forgive, and to love." When the occasion arises, it is good to talk to your little ones about patience, hope, and forgiveness.

On pages 36-37, before Communion, teach them to pray "O Lord, have mercy on me and allow me to receive Thy gifts!" and after, teach them to pray, "Glory to Thee, O Lord, glory to Thee," the words that begin the Prayers of Thanksgiving after Communion in an adult prayer book.

On page 39, you can teach them the Jesus prayer in the abbreviated form that even monastics sometimes use: "O Lord Jesus, have mercy on me!"

How to read this book to older, preschool-aged children

How should you present this book to preschool-aged children, aged 4 or 5, whose level of development is such that they are ready to absorb the full text of the book but who still don't know how to read, or at least how to read fluently? To start with, of course, like with all new books, you'll browse through the book with your child and look at the illustrations together. At this stage, it's just a book with pictures "about God." You can tell your children right away that this isn't a storybook, but a book of prayers, and that prayer is a conversation with God. As you look through the illustrations without hurrying, it's best to let your children speak and listen to them describe how they understand what they're seeing.

Then, we move on to reading the book. The introduction is actually written for the adults who read this book with their children (and once again, not just to their children but with their children). Make sure not to gloss over the introduction. It gives you what you need to move forward and begin to pray together.

Turning the page, the prayers themselves start. Here, you should stand and cross yourself (and ask your children to do the same) and then begin to pray with your children from the book. Soon, your children will begin to connect every turn of the page with the prayers that are written there and then it will truly be their prayer book.

The first time you read the book, take a pause after each page. You'll also need to watch for the moment when you'll need to stop and let your children go do something else for a while, perhaps until the end of the day or even tomorrow. Prayer takes concentration and work and it's important to let them rest.

You can use the little pauses as you flip through the book to look at the pictures again, to answer your children's questions, and perhaps, to talk to them about the prayers you have just prayed.

When you read the prayer book together with your children, that "reading" of the book (by memory and by the illustrations) will gradually turn into them praying and soon your joint prayers will no longer depend on actually reading the book.

It would be really good if you were able to sing some of the prayers with your children, like the "Our Father," "O Theotokos and Virgin," and "Lord, have mercy!" Try it! It is an active and joyful form of common prayer.

Explanations of the Prayers

We have tried to explain the contents of the prayers in words that children can understand although in a few cases, we've added a little bit to help parents understand more clearly as well.

"In the name of the Father, and the Son, and the Holy Spirit. Amen."
With these words, we begin our prayers and also every good work. We should always do everything for God, in His name. And Father, Son, and Holy Spirit is God's name!

As Orthodox Christians, we bear the name of our Lord Jesus Christ. He is our God. We also call Him the Son of God, the Son of God the Father. And the Holy Spirit is also true God. And all of them are one God, not three. The Holy Trinity, one and undivided. This is a great mystery that God has revealed about Himself to mankind. It is impossible to explain this mystery but God Himself helps those who love Him to understand and receive it with their hearts. All of the great saints who were filled with love for God praised the Holy Trinity.

"Glory to Thee, our God, glory to Thee.
Glory to the Father, and the Son, and the Holy Spirit, both now and ever and unto ages of ages. Amen."
With these words, we glorify and praise God. We also glorify Him when we say something shorter, every time we say "Glory to God!" which is also a prayer.

"Both now and ever and unto ages of ages. Amen."
This means today, forever, and in all ages, since God is eternal. He always has been, even when the earth and the whole universe didn't exist, even when time itself didn't exist, and He always will be and He will always be great and glorified.

Prayer to the Holy Spirit

"O heavenly King, O Comforter, the Spirit of truth, who art in all places and fillest all things; Treasury of good things and Giver of life: Come and dwell in us and cleanse us from every stain, and save our souls, O Good One."

When addressing someone, we often have special words that we use. For example, when we address the Holy Spirit, we call Him "Heavenly King," "the Comforter," and the "Spirit of truth." When we call Him "the Treasury of good things," that means that He is the source of everything good. We call Him the "Giver of life," since He gives life to everything and everyone. We also say that He is "in all places and fillest all things," since He is everywhere and fills everything with Himself. That means that He is present everywhere, supporting all things and helping all things attain the goal that God has set for them. That is why we ask Him to abide in us as well and to cleanse us from everything bad and to save us from evil.

The Trisagion

"Holy God, Holy Mighty, Holy Immortal, have mercy on us."

This prayer is one that people learned from angels and then added to it their human words, "Have mercy on us." When God has mercy on us, it means that He acts towards us according to His mercy and love.

The Lord's Prayer

Our Father, who art in Heaven, hallowed be Thy name. Thy Kingdom come. Thy will be done on earth as it is in Heaven. Give us this day our daily bread and forgive us our trespasses as we forgive those who trespass against us and lead us not into temptation but deliver us from the evil one.

This prayer is called the Lord's prayer because the Lord Jesus Christ Himself gave it to His disciples when they asked Him to teach them how to pray.

By beginning with the words "*Our Father*," we show that God allows us to come to Him as children to their Father.

"*Who art in Heaven*", because God abides in Heaven..

"*Hallowed be Thy name,*" shows our request to God that we might glorify Him by our words and actions.

"*Thy Kingdom come*," means that we want the Kingdom of God to come inside of us so that we might live according to His laws.

"*Thy will be done, on earth as it is in Heaven*," means that just like in Heaven, where the angels and saints do Thy will, so may Thy will be done here on the earth. When we ask this, we promise God that we'll do not what we want but what He expects from us.

"*Give us this day our daily bread*" doesn't just mean that we're asking Him for bread, but for everything necessary, everything that we can't do without in life. We're not just asking for what we need for our bodies but we're also asking for everything that our soul needs to live. That means Communion, prayer, and everything that is truly good and virtuous, that brings us closer to God.

"*And forgive us our trespasses as we forgive those who trespass against us.*" By trespasses, we mean the sins and offenses that we have committed against God. And those who trespass against us are those people who are guilty of anything against us, for example, by not treating us with love or by offending us. If we ask God to forgive us our trespasses, our sins, but we don't forgive others ourselves, then we will not receive forgiveness from God.

"*And lead us not into temptation.*" Temptations are those situations in life when it seems very easy to commit a sin and sometimes even seems impossible not to. For example, we might think that the only way to save ourselves from some misfortune or punishment is to tell a lie. Being tempted means being tested to see what we will choose: the difficult good or the easy evil. And we ask God to help us stand firm and choose what is good and not sin in any such temptation.

"*But deliver us from the evil one.*" Deliver us from evil and from the father of all evil, the devil.

Prayer to the Most-Holy Theotokos

"*O Virgin Theotokos, rejoice, O Mary, full of grace, the Lord is with Thee. Blessed art Thou among women and blessed is the fruit of Thy womb for Thou has born the Savior of our souls.*"

"*Full of grace*" means that she has received grace from God.

"*Blessed art Thou among women*" means that she is exalted among women.

"*The fruit of Thy womb*" is Jesus Christ, who was born from her.

"*For Thou has born the Savior of our souls.*" means that she has born the Lord Jesus Christ, who has saved our souls.

In this prayer, we praise the Mother of God and express our love for Her.

Prayer to Your Guardian Angel

"*O Angel of God, my holy guardian, sent to me by God from Heaven for my salvation! I fervently pray thee: Enlighten me this day and preserve me from all evil. Teach me to do what is good and lead me onto the path of salvation. Amen.*"

"*The path of salvation.*" God gives us His angels who are servants, ministering to us who are to receive salvation.

The Lord gives to all who are baptized a guardian angel who protects them from all evil, helps them to do good, and prays for them before God. Our angels are always with us. They see everything that we do and think, but they always see God and praise Him together with the other angels.

Prayer to the Saint Whose Name You Bear

"Pray to God for me, O holy God-pleasing Saint (Name), for I fervently run to thee, the speedy helper and intercessor for my soul."

"I fervently run to thee" means that, with all my heart, I turn to my angel for help.

At baptism, each of us is given the name of one of the saints. That saint, out of all the great multitude of saints, is then particularly close to us and becomes our own. We call that saint our "patron saint," and our intercessor before God (because that saint intercedes for us as an older brother or sister in the faith who loves us). We should call on our saint every day in prayer and we should try to read and try to imitate the saint's life.

Prayer for Your Parents
Prayer for the Living
Prayer for the Reposed

Turning to God with faith and love, we want to (and are obligated to) commemorate those who are close to us. We remember them ourselves and also ask God not to forget them. Of course, we should pray especially fervently for those who are the very closest to us: our mom and dad (and there's a separate prayer just for them) and for those we live with, for our close relatives, and our dear friends. We should definitely pray for our teachers and instructors, and for all those who help us every day (our benefactors). And of course, we should remember to pray for those who are having an especially difficult and hard time: those who are sick, suffering, and need help right now. We can't always help others with our deeds but we can always help them with our prayers. But the most difficult kind of prayer is also important. The Lord teaches us to pray for our enemies, for those who offend us and do evil against us. This is very important! And very difficult. But prayers for those who have offended us are very powerful. They bring love in place of evil. Often, from one such prayer, those who had been our enemies become our friends and those who were evil become good.

"For the Reposed" means for those who have died. We pray for them just like we pray for the living because, to God, all are living. The word "resposed" means "having fallen asleep." The dead have fallen asleep until the general resurrection when everyone who has died will come back to life and stand together before God. Their souls are alive even now but at that time, their bodies will arise as well. Right now, when earthly life has ended for them, our love for our beloved reposed can only be expressed in prayer, but they feel that prayer and it does a lot for them. We should teach children also to pray for their relatives and family benefactors that they don't remember but that they have heard of from their mom and dad. Those prayers themselves will bring those departed loved ones that they've only heard about closer to them and they'll grow to love them.

Our prayer for the reposed is also a prayer for us to meet them in the Kingdom of Heaven. Grant, O Lord, that we may be with Thee in the light of Thy love!

Closing Prayers

"It is truly meet to bless thee, O Theotokos, who art ever blessed and all-blameless, and the mother of our God. More honorable than the Cherubim, and more glorious beyond compare than the Seraphim, thou who without stain barest God the Word, and art truly Theotokos: we magnify thee.."

"It is truly meet" means that it is fitting and appropriate.

"All-blameless" means without any spot, fully without sin.

"Cherubim and seraphim" are the highest angels, closest to God.

"Without stain" means without any sin or pain.

"Thou gavest birth to God the Word" or, in other words, to the Son

of God, Jesus Christ.

"*True Theotokos,*" for she is truly the one who bore God.

Prayer After Eating

"*...but as Thou didst come to Thy disciples, O Savior, and grant them peace, so come to us and save us!*"

When Christ rose from the dead, He appeared to His disciples. "Jesus Himself stood in the midst of them, and said to them, 'Peace to you'" and then He took the fish that the disciples gave Him and the honeycomb and "He took it and ate in their presence." (Luke 24:36, 43). We call the Lord Jesus Christ to be invisibly present with us, as well.

Prayer After Finishing a Task

"Thou art the fulfillment of all good things, O my Christ. Fill my soul with joy and gladness and save me, since Thou alone art most merciful, O Lord, glory to Thee."

"Since Thou alone art most merciful." Because you, O Christ, are the only one who is truly full of mercy.

Prayer of the Elders of Optina

At the right time, you can tell your children about the Optina Hermitage, a monastery on the shore of the Zhizdra River that was home to remarkable monks called "elders," not so much because of their age as because they were very wise and good and revealed to people the will of God and taught them to love God and how to pray to Him. They composed this prayer.

A Prayer Before Communion

"Of Thy Mystical Supper, O Son of God, receive me today as a communicant for I will not speak of Thy Mysteries to Thine enemy nor will I give Thee a kiss like Judas but like the thief I will confess Thee: Remember me, O Lord, in Thy Kingdom."

"Thy Mystical Supper," refers to the last supper that the Lord Jesus Christ had with His disciples, where He called them His friends, blessed bread and wine and said that it was His body and blood and that, when they tasted these gifts, they would be united with Him and would receive the forgiveness of their sins.

"Communicant." A communicant is one who receives the Eucharist and is united thereby with God.

"I will not speak of Thy Mysteries to Thine enemy" means that I will not betray this Holy Mystery, these sacred things, to Christ's enemies.

"Nor will I give Thee a kiss like Judas." I will not give Christ a false kiss like Judas the betrayer did.

"But like the thief I will confess Thee: Remember me, O Lord, in Thy Kingdom." Children can learn the meaning of these words of the Wise Thief on the cross, about the betrayal of Judas, and about the Mystical Supper from the book, "The Resurrection of Christ" in this same series of books.

If your children commune at Church, they hear this prayer before Holy Communion, either while the clergy are communing or when the priest comes out with the Chalice with the Holy Gifts and they might also hear the next prayer, the prayer of thanksgiving after communion at the end of Liturgy, if it's read aloud for all the people at your parish.

In explaining the Eucharist to your children, you can tell them that it's a sacred food that God gives us, just like He once gave to His disciples at the Mystical Supper. When we receive Communion, God's love permeates us and we become like He is.

www.ingramcontent.com/pod-product-compliance
Lightning Source LLC
Chambersburg PA
CBHW040003080526
44586CB00027B/2867